This is a landmark book. It teaches people who want to reach Muslims—but who are not aware of the sensitive issues—to understand what it takes to reach these dear people. For those of us whose hearts have been touched by the cry of those unreached millions, this book is refreshing and challenging. Islam is on the rise and is advancing all over the world. This book is a must for any person who wants to reach Muslims anywhere they are found.
                                                    –Jacqueline Hajjar, Ph.D.
                                    Professor, Lebanese American University

A Muslim's Heart *is a concise and positive resource to begin learning how to relate to Muslims.*

                                                    –Paul Martindale
                                                    Arab World Ministries

Dr. Hoskins has given us a most helpful and practical introduction to the beliefs and cultural mindset of Muslims. Dr. Hoskins is motivated by a profound love for Jesus Christ and an abiding passion to see Muslims, made in the image of God, surrender their lives to the Savior. To that end, may this book be a powerful tool.
                                        –Pastor Michael L. Andrakowicz
                                        Berean Baptist Church, Sacramento, CA

A Muslim's Heart *is a great, practical summary of how to connect spiritually with your Muslim friends. Though short, it covers the basics needed to understand and relate, not just on a theological level but with the cultural heart of your friend. When I'm asked for a good place to start by someone wanting to relate to their Muslim friends and coworkers, I recommend this book.*
                    –Paul, area director with an overseas missions agency

I have used many of the "relational tips" from this book in both my professional and social interactions with Muslims. I have seen their openness to hearing my story about my relationship with Jesus and have experienced the willingness of Muslims to reach out to the heart of God and the heart of man.
                                                    –Professor Richard H. Grant

A MUSLIM'S HEART

What Every Christian Needs to Know to Share Christ with Muslims

By Dr. Edward J. Hoskins

NAVPRESS

For a free catalog
of NavPress books & Bible studies call
1-800-366-7788 (USA) or 1-800-839-4769 (Canada).

www.NavPress.com

The Navigators is an international Christian organization. Our mission is to
advance the gospel of Jesus and His kingdom into the nations through spiritual generations of laborers living and discipling among the lost. We see a vital
movement of the gospel, fueled by prevailing prayer, flowing freely through
relational networks and out into the nations where workers for the kingdom are
next door to everywhere.

NavPress is the publishing ministry of The Navigators. The mission of NavPress
is to reach, disciple, and equip people to know Christ and make Him known
by publishing life-related materials that are biblically rooted and culturally relevant. Our vision is to stimulate spiritual transformation through every product
we publish.

© 2003, 2005 Edward J. Hoskins.

ISBN-10: 0-9672480-6-X
ISBN-13: 978-0-96724-806-6

All Scriptures are taken from the *Holy Bible: New International Version®* (NIV®).
Copyright © 1973, 1978, 1984 by International Bible Society. All Qur'anic pas-
sages are from *The Koran Interpreted,* a translation by A.J. Arberry, © 1955 by
George Allen & Unwin Ltd.

Printed in the United States of America.

3 4 5 6 7 8 / 11 10 09 08

DEDICATION

This book is dedicated to the many Kingdom laborers currently serving in God's harvest fields among the House of Islam. This is for Uncle B, who believed in me and has encouraged me over the years. This is for K, who first instructed me in Kingdom principles and spiritual warfare. This is for D, who taught me my first Arabic proverbs. This is for N and I, Arab national believers: May your humility and learner spirits continue to bear fruit long after we "short-term foreigners" have left the field. This is for the family of Rev. F: As your father once exhorted me, "May it be done to you according to your faith." This is for the 3 M's: May your freezer-wrap plan outlast the 40 years. This is for my two children: May your heritage flourish like the cedars of Lebanon. Finally, this book is dedicated to my wife. She refused to have her name appear as coauthor, although no one was more deserving. May the Lord give you your "hundred" and grant your request to influence the next 10 generations for Him. I salute each and every one of you. Maranatha!

ACKNOWLEDGMENT

I would like to express my deepest gratitude to the staff of Dawson Media for making this book a reality.

CONTENTS

FOREWORD

IT WAS MY FIRST EXPERIENCE DISCUSSING the Bible with Muslims on their own turf. I was in Jordan, visiting friends. One of them, K, invited me to go with him to a Muslim home where he had been meeting with a family to explore the life of Jesus.

The two of us walked across town into a neighborhood of flat-roofed, one-story houses, all of them the same yellowish-gray color as the dusty street beneath our feet. We arrived at the house and knocked on the door.

K had prepared me for what might happen next. He told me that if just the elder son appeared, it was a signal that the situation wasn't really safe. But if the father and brother were also present, we could go ahead with our Bible discussion. And if the mother was also there to greet us, it would signal that we were especially welcome.

The door opened and there stood the three men. They invited us in. As we entered, the mother came out of the kitchen to greet us. I glanced down the little hallway to see five small, covered heads peeking around a corner. That was all we got to see or hear of their children that afternoon.

We found ourselves in a living room, sparsely furnished with a sofa, a few chairs, and a low table in the center of the room. As we sat down, the mother entered with a pitcher full of a cool fruit drink and some glasses. She placed them on the table and disappeared back into the kitchen. A few minutes passed while we made small talk. Then the mother appeared again, this time with a platter of fresh dates. When she left it was time to get into our discussion.

K began by narrating one of Jesus' parables about the kingdom of God. (How else would you do it in a place where it is unsafe to carry a Bible?) We talked about possible meanings of the parable.

K narrated another similar parable, and then another, while platters of fruit and pastries were regularly supplied by the mother. Suddenly there was a knock on the door. It opened before anyone could get up, and in walked a family cousin. Scarcely pausing to begin a new sentence, the father switched subjects—a discussion of the state of education in the country. Since K was an educator, the father knew that would be a safe subject. The cousin never got a clue as to what was really going on in that room before he stepped in.

As we walked away I was painfully aware of how clumsy I had felt in that home. I knew signals were going on all the time that I couldn't read. At that moment, the gap between their Arab culture and my Western culture seemed insurmountable. How does one find enough common ground for meaningful communication to occur, I wondered.

That was 20 years ago. Since then I have had other similar experiences. The gap is narrowing, but I know it will never disappear for me. I still struggle with the same feelings of foreign-ness, even as I pick my way through my local shopping mall and cross paths with a Muslim family, the mother and daughter in their headscarves and their dresses to the floor. I'm tempted to just keep to my world and leave them to theirs. But I can't do that. Jesus' parting words to us closes the door on that idea: "Go and make disciples of all nations" (Matthew 28:19). Today, one person in five is Muslim. So I'll catch the father's eye, smile, and say, "hello." I love it when I get a response! Little beginnings can have big outcomes.

It is our move. It's not up to them to close this cultural gap. It's up to us. (Certainly many Muslims now living in this country must feel as ill at ease in our culture as I did in theirs.) The apostle Paul put it this way: "To the Jews I became like a Jew, to win the Jews. To those under the law I became like those under the law . . . so as to win those under the law. To the weak I became weak, to win the weak. . . . I do all this for the sake of the gospel that I might share in its blessing" (1 Corinthians 9:20–23). In other words, it's the responsibility of the messengers to adapt their lifestyle to those they are communicating with in order to help them feel comfortable. That's scary, but that's the way it is. But how do we do that?

Ed Hoskins and I have been friends for years. With great admiration, I have watched Ed and his family make themselves at home in several Middle Eastern countries. In this book, he helps us immeasurably with this challenge of closing the gap between the Arab and Western cultures. He writes with the authority of an eyewitness. Now Ed has given us the distilled essence of what they have learned over a lifetime in 60 short pages. I know of no other book like this one.

–Jim Petersen
Coauthor of *The Insider: Bringing the*
Kindom of God into Your Everyday World

INTRODUCTION

"OF MAKING MANY BOOKS THERE IS NO END, and much study wearies the body" (Ecclesiastes 12:11). In one sense, these words reflect my reluctance to write this guide. Is another book on reaching Muslims with the Gospel really necessary? In another sense, the events of September 11, 2001, have given an increased urgency for understanding and reaching out to our Muslim friends and neighbors. For 30 years I have had a passion to know my Lord and Savior Jesus Christ in ever-increasing depth and to make Him known to others. For more than 20 of those 30 years, my driving force has been to understand Islam with the purpose of helping Muslims see and meet Jesus Christ.

The good news is that Muslims *can* enter God's eternal Kingdom and have new life in Christ. They can be completely, ceremonially, and permanently cleansed from all unrighteousness and no longer need to wonder whether or not they will be one of those admitted to paradise. Yes, the Messiah Jesus came not only for Jews and Christians, but also for Muslims and for every other people group in the world.

Since the early 1970s, I have felt called by God to be involved with restricted-access people (those primarily in the "10/40 window"). In 1980 I moved to Beirut, Lebanon, with my wife and two small children to teach biology at a local college. There I became affiliated with an international, nondenominational disciplemaking organization.

Since that time, my family and I have lived among Muslims overseas and at home in the United States. It's been a great privilege to see, hear, and do things most believers will never experience. I've lived through a civil war, had my life threatened, met royalty, and discipled believers in an underground church. I've bargained in local markets, attended a public flogging (originally scheduled as a beheading), eaten lamb in a Bedouin tent, enjoyed at least a thousand hours drinking tea, and even confronted demons! Through all this, I've met hundreds of friendly Muslims who have taught me much more about God, life, and people.

Over these 20-plus years, the Lord has allowed me and my family to relate deeply and share the Gospel and Scriptures with more than 100 Muslims from at least 20 different North African, Middle Eastern, and Asian countries. They have come from all walks of life, from top-level executives to Bedouin tribesmen, from doctors to taxicab drivers, plus women and children. I would like to share some of the people, stories, and lessons from my journey with you.

This guide is intended primarily for someone who knows some basic facts about Muslims, but doesn't know what to do with them. It is for the college student who meets Muslims at school and wants to begin talking about matters of faith. It is for the long- or short-term missionary who will work with Muslims either here or abroad. It's for the woman who wants to reach out to the wife of an international student or the family with Muslim neighbors. It is for the university professor who has Muslim students in her class, for seminary students training for ministerial careers, and for pastors who want to help their congregations navigate the tricky waters of interacting with Muslims. In short, this guide is for any Christian who has Muslim friends, neighbors, or coworkers and wants to introduce them to Jesus.

Those of us who have hearts for Muslims have been greatly served by pioneers in the field of Muslim ministry. However, the average Christian is not a pioneer. While they may learn from the writing and teaching of these pioneers, they don't know how to put the information into practice. The average Christian, I believe, needs the cookies placed on the lower shelf, just as I did when I began ministering more than 20 years ago.

Over time, I have experienced some breakthroughs in understanding and relating to Muslims, especially in sharing the Gospel with them in practical and culturally relevant ways. This gives me hope. My goal for this guide is to give hope to others, too.

My recommendation is that you not read this book straight through like a novel. Instead, scroll through the table of contents, pick a topic that is of immediate interest, and start there.

You will not find these pages filled with missionary success stories. Over the years I have seen four (not 40 or 400) Muslims place their faith in Christ as a result of their interaction with me. One I have lost contact with, one is a pastor, one is an executive, and one completed his Ph.D. and went on to a governmental position. With the exception of the last person, at my most recent contact, they were all continuing to grow in their love relationship with Christ and sharing their joy with others. The last person was severely tormented by his family and friends and eventually returned to fundamentalist Islam. The final verdict is still out on his situation. Yet each of these friends gives me great delight and courage to persevere!

I have received many requests from Christians with Muslim friends who ask, "Can you give me some advice on how to take the next step in sharing Jesus with my friends?" It is that advice that I share in this book. I have tried to be candid about my errors as well as what has worked. May you profit from both.

ISLAM 101

ON A FRIDAY AFTERNOON, white-robed men with untrimmed beards file out of the local mosque. Smells from a restaurant advertise chicken biryani. Children play while women in headscarves exchange news with friends. Bits of conversation in Arabic, Indonesian, and Urdu can be overheard. Welcome to Indiana.

With minor variations, this scene is being played out in Chicago and Chattanooga, in Los Angeles and Lafayette. Witness the emerging face of Islam in America.

If you're picking up this book, it's probably because you're part of one of these communities. Maybe your casual acquaintances with Muslim neighbors or coworkers—not to mention the events of September 11—are driving you to ask deeper questions about Muslims. What do they believe and why? How do we answer their claims? How do we relate to them? How can we effectively live out the Gospel with them? What can we learn from them?

In answer to these questions, I challenge you with the words of the Master, "Come and see!"

WHAT IS ISLAM AND WHO ARE MUSLIMS?
"Islam" is an Arabic word meaning "surrender" or "submission." It is a religion embraced by one-fifth of the world's population. A person who follows the religion of Islam is called a Muslim. A person becomes a Muslim by reciting the following creed: "There is no God but Allah, and Muhammad is the messenger of Allah."

IS ALLAH GOD?
Some Christians believe and teach that Allah is not the same as God, and that when Muslims say the word "Allah" they are not

referring to the one true God. Our response to this issue has significant missiological and theological implications. If we say that Allah is God, are we encouraging idol worship? If we use a different word than "Allah," where is our common ground, our starting point for introducing them to Jesus?

The main difficulty with asking "Is Allah God?" is that it is really two questions. The first is linguistic: Can we legitimately use the word "Allah" for God in relating and witnessing to our Muslim friends? The second is theological: Is the character of Allah taught in traditional Islam the same as that taught about God in the Bible? If the answer to the second question is "no," do we need to find another word besides "Allah" when we speak about God to Muslims?

Linguistically, the word "Allah" comes from the Arabic *Al-Ilah*, meaning "The God."[1, 2] It has the Semitic root, *ilah*, corresponding to the Hebrew *eloah* (singular form of the more familiar plural *Elohim*)[2]. "Allah" is the word for God currently used in the Arabic Bible and has been reverently used by many millions of Arab Christians since the first century A.D.

By way of contrast, the Greek translation of our own word for God (*theos*) actually has a "heathen" Greek origin[3] with an Indo-European root, *dhes*.[2] The pagan Greek Zeus has the Indo-European root of *dyeu* and is the origin of *Deus* ("God" in the Latin Vulgate Bible), *Dios* (Spanish), and *Dieu* (French).[2] Finally, our English word "God" comes from the proto-Germanic pagan word for a god or idol. It was neutral in gender until it was masculinized by Germanic tribes who converted to Christianity in the mid-first millennium A.D.[1]

In fact, Arab Christians may well have a better case for not wanting to translate their word "Allah" into the English "God" for fear that our word has pagan origins! They might just as well ask, "Is God Allah?"

The theological question is more difficult to tackle. It is clear that many similarities exist between the God of Judaism and Christianity, and Islam's Allah. Both Muslims and Christians believe that God is the Creator of heaven and earth, that He is all

2

powerful and all knowing, and that He communicates to human beings through His spoken and written word. Both Christianity and Islam have angels, prophets, and a final day of judgment, which includes a literal heaven and hell. But there are also significant differences.

Islam's Allah is totally "other," transcendent, and uniquely "one." As a result, no person or object can ever represent Allah or show others what he is like. He is therefore unknowable and free, being bound by nothing—not rules, covenants, or even his own word. In Islam, Allah has 99 names, but not one of them is sacrificial *agape* love. Muslims recognize sin but not the concept of original sin. Forgiveness exists, but it's based on Allah's unpredictable decree and not on any absolute standard or justice. Because sin does not need to be paid for, there is no need for atonement, a savior, or a cross.

To Christians, it is clear that the Islamic portrayal of Allah is, at best, inadequate; at worst, it's inaccurate, negating the centrality of Christ. But think about this: **Since when does a people group's inaccurate concept of God require us to use a different word for Him?** What about the millions of Americans who have an incorrect view of God? Do we need to use a different word for God with them? More important, what about the 15 million Arabic-speaking Christians who use the word "Allah" for God? In relating to Muslims, it is not the word for God (or Allah) that needs to be changed, but their concept of who God is.

THE FIVE PILLARS OF ISLAM
Classical Islam is based on five foundations, called "pillars," which include the witness, prayer, giving alms, fasting, and pilgrimage. In addition, *jihad* is sometimes included as a sixth pillar. An explanation of each pillar follows.

The witness—Shahada (sha-HAA-da)
Meaningfully saying (in Arabic), "There is no God but Allah, and Muhammad is the messenger of Allah" is all it takes to become a Muslim. This phrase, the *shahada*, is the most frequently repeated

sentence in Islam and is spoken daily during prayers and at other times. It is the first thing whispered into the ear of a newborn Muslim baby and the last thing heard and spoken at death.

Prayer—Salat (sa-LAAT)
Muslims pray facing Mecca (a city in southwestern Saudi Arabia) five times a day: dawn, noon, mid-afternoon, sunset, and late evening. Before they pray, Muslims must ritually cleanse certain parts of their bodies—hands, arms to the elbows, face, head and scalp, ears, nose, and feet to the ankles—with water; this is known as *wuthu* (wuu-DTHUU). As they pray, Muslims assume special prayer positions at special times, including standing respect-fully (with arms folded), kneeling prostrate (with nose, forehead, hands, knees, and the bottoms of the feet all touching the prayer rug), kneeling while sitting up, and bending over at the waist. As they go through these prayer positions, specific memorized prayers are repeated that include portions from their holy book, the Qur'an (kuur-AAN).

Praying may be done individually, but whenever possible, it is done in a group with one respected Muslim leading the prayers. After praying, they turn toward their right and left shoulders and speak the Muslim greeting, "Peace be upon you" (as-sa-LAAM-uu a-LAY-kuum), addressing first the angel who records their good deeds (the one who sits on their right shoulder) and then the one who records their bad deeds (on their left shoulder).

Men and women do not pray together. Women can go to the mosque, but there is always a separate room for them.

Giving alms/Charity—Zakat (za-KAAT)
Muslims are expected to give two-and-a-half percent of their income to charity. Often, this takes the form of food—feeding beggars who come to the door or paying for sacrificial animals during Ramadan for those who can't afford them.

Fasting—Soum/Siyam (SOWM, see-YAAM)
When physically possible, every adult Muslim is expected to

fast—abstaining from eating, drinking, smoking, swallowing saliva, and sexual intercourse—from dawn until dusk during the entire ninth lunar Islamic month of Ramadan. This is the month when Muslims believe Allah caused the Qur'an to descend from heaven and gave it verbally to Muhammad. (The lunar year is approximately 11 days shorter than the solar year, which we follow in the United States. For this reason, Ramadan does not occur at the same time each year. The dates change, falling about 11 days earlier in each consecutive year.) When the month-long fast ends, there is a three-day celebration that includes singing, dancing, visiting, gift-giving, and often fireworks. It is possibly the biggest, most joyful event in a Muslim's year.

Pilgrimage—Hajj

Once in his or her lifetime, every Muslim is expected, if physically and financially able, to make a pilgrimage to Mecca. This involves a complex set of rituals as they reenact Muhammad's flight (or pilgrimage) from Mecca to the nearby city of Medina.

Jihad (jee-HAAD)

Jihad is sometimes included as a sixth pillar. It is less frequently discussed and is often misunderstood, especially by Westerners. Jihad **simply means "struggle," but it can be interpreted in various ways.** It certainly denotes an internal struggle as a person strives against his or her own sinful nature or bad habits while try-ing to gain religious merit. (Western Christians call this a struggle against "the flesh.") A second form of jihad is the struggle within Islam to better the community (through education, for example). It can also mean external struggle (outside Islam) against anyone or any group that threatens the safety of Islam or Muslims. The most extreme interpretation comes when a respected Muslim leader believes that all Islam is in danger and calls for a gen-eral jihad, or holy war, to be fought against "unbelievers" (non-Muslims). This is not, however, the most common meaning of jihad. Most Muslims tell me that the first two are the primary interpretations.

THE LIFE OF MUHAMMAD

In A.D. 570, Muhammad was born into the family of Banu Hashim. The Banu Hashim, a clan of the larger Quraish tribe, are believed to be descended from Abraham's son Ishmael.

Muhammad's father died on a caravan journey before his son was born, and so the young boy was raised by his grandfather. When his grandfather died, Muhammad's uncle Abu-Talib, then head of the Banu Hashim clan, raised him. Muhammad did not inherit wealth, but he served as the business agent and caravan leader for a wealthy older widow named Khadija. They were married when he was 25 and she was 40. They had six children, but only the girls survived. Khadija died in A.D. 619.

Muhammad, who was appalled at the idol worship prevalent in his day, was in the habit of meditating each evening. Muslims believe that in the year A.D. 610, while he meditated in a cave outside Mecca, Muhammad was visited by the angel Jibreel (Gabriel), who commanded Muhammad to "Recite!" After several commands, Muhammad memorized what the angel told him and then repeated these messages to his family and friends. Throughout the remainder of his life (he died in A.D. 632 at age 62), Muhammad received numerous other revelations. These were compiled into the Qur'an, which means "recitation."

By the year A.D. 613, Muhammad was publicly preaching his message from Allah, telling the people of Mecca to submit and surrender to Allah. He called for a stop to idol worship, denounced selfishness and materialism, and warned people of the coming "Day of Judgment."

Some listened and submitted, but most did not. With opposition growing, Muhammad finally fled from Mecca to the larger city of Medina, 200 miles to the north. This year, A.D. 622, marks the beginning of the Islamic calendar and is commemorated annually by the Hajj (pilgrimage). The people of Medina warmly received him and his teaching, and many became Muslims. For the next eight years, extensive warring took place between the Muslims of Medina and the idol-worshipers of Mecca, who finally surrendered the city in A.D. 630. By the time of Muhammad's death two years later, all of Arabia had "surrendered" to Allah.

Most Muslims at that time believed one of Muhammad's first converts, Abu-Bakr (who was already recognized as Muhammad's second-in-command), had been instructed by Muhammad to take over the Islamic leadership—to become the first *caliph* (ka-LEEF)—after his death. Others believed that Muhammad's son-in-law Ali should be given the leadership because he was the closest male relative. (Remember that none of Muhammad's sons survived to adulthood.) Ali was not only related to Muhammad by marriage but was also his cousin. Ali's supporters, angry at this snub, were later known as the "party of Ali." In Arabic, the word for party is *shia* (SHEE-aa), and Ali's followers were known as *Shiites* (SHEE-ites). The followers of the traditional caliphate of Abu-Bakr became known as *Sunnis* (SUUN-neez). (The caliphate, or succession of recognized leaders in Islam, remained until the early twentieth century and ended with the Turkish Ottoman Empire.)

This distinction continues today. Iran is roughly 93 percent Shiite, while Iraq is about half and half. Most of the rest of the Islamic world is Sunni. Major differences exist between the two groups. Their view of leadership and spiritual revelation is different. For example, the Shiites recognized the Ayatollah Khomeini as Islam's leader and spokesman, but the Sunnis did not. Shiites believe that their top religious leader speaks for God today, while Sunnis believe that God spoke only in the Qur'an, and the revelation is a closed canon. One Sunni friend of mine was convinced that Shiites were not true Muslims because "when they pray, they hold their arms different from us." Some Shiites even add an additional phrase to the end of the traditional witness. As a rule, the two groups mistrust each other and do not intermix.

AN OVERVIEW OF THE QUR'AN

According to Muslim scholars, the Qur'an is a compilation of revelations that were believed to be given over a period of 22 years. It was primarily memorized but was also written down on animal skins, palm leaves, and flat animal bones such as shoulder blades. During Muhammad's lifetime and after his death, many of the followers memorized the entire Qur'an, which is about the length of the Bible's New Testament. In one major battle, more than 70 of these "memorizers" of the Qur'an were killed, and it was feared the Qur'an might be completely lost. As a result, in the time of the third caliph Uthman (approximately 15 to 20 years after the death of Muhammad) the Qur'an was formally collated. During this process, "variant readings" of the Qur'an were found. Subsequently, all copies and fragments were gathered. The most reliable one was chosen, and the rest were burned.[4] Every Qur'an since that time is believed to be identical to the one that was spared.

Christianity has many early copies and fragments (almost 25,000) of the Bible still in existence, some dating to within 100 years of the time of Christ. This delights scholars because even the variant readings give clues and support to the overall integrity of our Scriptures. One Muslim privately admitted to a friend of mine that "this is one of the biggest problems we as Muslims face—we don't have those burned manuscripts!" Although not discussed openly, from a textual criticism and scholarly viewpoint, the decision to destroy the variant readings was disastrous.

From these humble beginnings, Islam has grown to encompass one-fifth of the world's population. **Approximately 4 million Muslims reside in the United States[5]**; Detroit alone is home to 250,000 Muslims. They worship in at least 200 U.S. mosques—one in virtually every major U.S. city.

Now that we've looked at the basics of Islam, let's try to understand the hearts and minds of its followers.

1. Weekley, Earnest. *An Etymological Dictionary of Modern English:Volume I.* New York: Dover Publications, 1967.
2. *The American Heritage Dictionary of the English Language: 4th edition.* Houghton-Mifflin Company, 2000.
3. Zodhiates, Spiros. *The Complete Word Study Dictionary: New Testament.* Chattanooga: AMG Publications, 1992.
4. From *The Translation of the Meanings of Sahih Al-Bukhari: Arabic-English* by Dr. Muhammad Muhsin Khan.
5. Fienberg, Howard and Murray, Iain. "How Many U.S. Muslims? Our Best Estimate," *Christian Science Monitor*, Nov. 29, 2001.

THE MUSLIM WORLDVIEW

A "WORLDVIEW" IS THE WAY PEOPLE SEE and process their environment. If you want to understand why people are the way they are, uncovering their worldview is a good place to start. The way people view their world will largely determine their decisions, allegiances, and actions.

Three driving forces impact a Muslim's worldview: the Bedouin ideal, honor, and Islamic traditions.

THE BEDOUIN IDEAL

Bedouin (BED-uu-win) is an Arabic term meaning "one who wanders" and is very important in Muslim culture. A Muslim views the rural, wandering Bedouin a little like Westerners picture the cowboy of the early American West. Bedouin men and women are admired, emulated, and lionized. Dr. Sania Hamady[1] characterizes the ideal Bedouin as bold, chivalrous, proud, sentimental, pious, and honorable. They are free—unbound by most restrictions and limited only by their own strength—as well as ceremonial, decent, dignified, and true to their promise. They are discrete, ascetic, generous, grateful, obedient to parents, loyal to friends and relatives, and honoring of the elderly. They are firm, stable, patient, and persevering. Nearly all Muslims strive to live up to these standards.

HONOR AND SHAME

Honor is the ship that floats all of Muslim culture. It is more important than logic, truth, and even life itself. This may seem odd to us in the West, but **honor is an actual commodity to Muslims, which can be bought and sold, added to, and sub-**

tracted from. An honorable family will be able to arrange more lucrative marriages, get better jobs, and have more important friends. Anything that adds to family honor (education, wealth, generosity) is highly valued. Anything that subtracts, namely shame, is to be avoided at all costs; female sexual immorality and changing religions top the list.

WORLDVIEW CONTRASTS

The following chart lists some of the most significant cultural values that impact a person's worldview and contrasts the Eastern world from the Western one.

Cultural Value	Eastern/Muslim Society	Western Society
Time orientation	Past (traditions)	Future
Time usage	Punctuality not important	Punctuality very important
Honor	All important	Helpful, but not essential
Status	Usually inherited	Usually earned
Change	Little value (often shunned)	Highly valued
Rights	Society is most important	Individual is most important
Relationships	People more important than events	Events often more important than people
Sin	An external mistake	An internal moral failure
Family	Extended	Nuclear, immediate
Aging	Leads to greater respect, increased decision-making	Usually leads to less respect and decision-making
Discipline	External (shame, by family)	Internal (physical, by parents)
Blame	Avoided, transferred	OK to accept blame
Confrontation	Usually indirect (third person or through a story)	Usually direct (first person, "cut to the chase")
Hospitality	Essential and honorable	Nice, but not essential

It's helpful to compare and contrast these values. Specific examples will shed even more light.

Time

When I moved to Lebanon, I was advised not to show up for an appointment exactly on time. I was told only servants do that.

Arriving 15 to 30 minutes after the appointed time, even for dinner, was considered acceptable, even preferable.

Honor

A Jordanian Bedouin friend provided me with a powerful example of the role of honor and shame in Muslim culture. One day he was at home when his father was struck and killed by a car. My friend grabbed his gun and chased the driver, who naturally fled. If my friend had caught up with him, it would have been within his "rights" to shoot him. (Instead, a third party later intervened to bring about restitution.) He knew that all society anticipated his attempt to catch and take revenge on his father's killer. It was the honorable thing to do. My friend also knew that the killer would flee. Both parties reacted exactly as expected.

Another friend instructed me that if I was ever involved in a serious car accident in the Middle East, I should immediately drive away. If the car wouldn't drive, I was to "get out and run." If I was caught, I was told, "Deny everything."

Relationships and hospitality

My wife and I were invited to a Lebanese family's home for dinner at 7:00 p.m. Shortly before we were to leave our house, another Lebanese couple showed up to visit us. Spontaneous visits are a compliment because they mean that the visitors view you as good friends. But we were expected at another family's house! My wife privately asked me, "What are we going to do?" Fortunately, I had just heard of a similar incident from other Westerners. I was told it would be impolite to get up and leave visitors, even if we explained that we had another engagement. Remember, people are more important than events. The family who originally invited us would understand; if we were late, they would assume someone else had dropped in. We weren't able to get word to them because our phone did not work, so we did nothing. We relaxed, enjoyed our surprise visitors, and later saw our other friends, who were very understanding about why we were late.

Confrontation

For a Muslim, preserving honor ("saving face") is top priority. This is especially true when conveying sensitive information. In Islamic culture, confrontation is done either through a third party or by telling a story (or, more likely, a series of stories for emphasis). While teaching in Lebanon, I caught two students cheating on an exam. Later, one of the students, accompanied by her fiancé, came to my house for "a visit." Over the next few hours, the fiancé politely told three stories, each of which I was able to place myself in. The first story went something like this: "We heard about a professor who caught some students cheating, and when he refused to change the grade, he was killed. Wasn't that terrible?" Later in the evening there were two other stories with some variation on the same theme (such as being beaten instead of killed). Did I get the message? You bet I did!

The story gets stranger. Shortly afterward, another student informed me that the whole class had actually cheated when I left the room for a few minutes. When I asked why they all cheated, I was informed that it was my fault. Incredulous, I asked why. I was told, "If you didn't want us to cheat, then it was your responsibility to keep us from cheating." This incident taught me a huge cultural lesson about blame and personal responsibility.

Sin

Sin is not taken as seriously in the East as it is in the West. Although it is considered wrong for a Muslim to sin, it is not nearly as bad as the shame of committing sin and then getting caught. Sin is relative and largely external ("What if someone sees what I did and tells others?") as opposed to the Western view of sin, which is more internal ("What do I do about the guilt I feel because of my moral failure?").

As I scratched my head over this, I began to notice some patterns. The big issue in the Muslim world is not sin, but cleanliness. Muslims place tremendous emphasis on becoming and maintaining ritual cleanliness, especially before prayer. Is there any parallel in our Western culture? Fortunately, yes. Our own

Old Testament deals extensively with cleanliness (see Leviticus 5:2–3, 7, 19–21; 10:10). In fact, nearly the entire book of Leviticus speaks to this issue.

BRIDGING EASTERN AND WESTERN WORLDVIEWS

While a Muslim worldview may seem completely foreign to a Western Christian, the Old Testament can serve as our bridge. As I looked at more of these cultural values, I came to realize that the Old Testament Hebrew culture is almost point-by-point in line with the Muslim worldview. If this is accurate, then we have a complete handbook in our own Bible to help us understand the Eastern worldview. (Why should it surprise us that God has provided this for us?)

Let me give an example. In his farewell address to the Israelites, Moses downplayed the real reason God didn't allow him to enter the Promised Land:

> "At that time I pleaded with the LORD: 'O Sovereign LORD, you have begun to show to your servant your greatness and your strong hand. For what god is there in heaven or on earth who can do the deeds and mighty works you do? Let me go over and see the good land beyond the Jordan—that fine hill country and Lebanon.' **But because of you** the LORD was angry with me and would not listen to me. 'That is enough,' the LORD said. 'Do not speak to me anymore about this matter' " (Deuteronomy 3:23–26, emphasis added).

Two other times in Deuteronomy, Moses makes this same statement, putting the blame on the Israelites instead of himself. But we know the real reason why Moses was not allowed to enter the Promised Land. He disobeyed God by striking the rock when he was commanded only to speak to it (Numbers 20:6–12). So was Moses lying? No, anyone from an Eastern background knows this. He was simply not accepting public blame—completely understandable from an Eastern worldview.

The Bible is not a Western book. Yes, it is pan-cultural, and the truths apply to all peoples, but the origins, stories, and forms are Eastern. Studying our own Bible with new, "Eastern" eyes can help us share the Gospel more effectively with our Muslim friends, and it can help us better know our own Bible. I make use of this fact and often ask my Muslim friends to "please help me understand my book better." They are usually pleased to assist.

---

1. *Temperament and Character of the Arabs*. Twayne Publishers, New York: 1960.

CHAPTER 3

RELATIONAL TIPS

AS FOLLOWERS OF CHRIST, we have been given the mandate to go to others with the message of salvation and new life in Christ (Matthew 28:19–20; Romans 15:20–21). This requires adaptation and flexibility, and it takes effort (1 Corinthians 9:19–23).

It also leads to some fundamental questions. Where is the balance as we seek to "become all things to all men . . . for the sake of the gospel" (1 Corinthians 9:22–23)? How far do we go to culturally adapt? How much contextualization is enough? How much is too much? These questions may be resolved by prayer, study, adherence to Scripture, instruction from more mature believers, and a heavy dose of the character of God.

It's also important to understand as much as you can about Muslims and their culture. For that reason, I offer this short course in relating to Muslims.

GREETINGS
Greetings between Easterners and Westerners can be tricky. In general, follow the lead of your Muslim friend and attempt to understand their different types of greetings.

Shaking hands
Shaking hands is a polite greeting in the East, just as it is in the West. However, never shake with your left hand. This is the hand used for "unclean" functions; extending it to others is considered an insult. Only twice in my life has a Muslim reached out his left hand to me. A child once offered me his left hand, and I rightly refused to shake it. Other children standing around him cried out "ha-RAM" (shame) to him. The second time, a new friend in

the Middle East had his right hand full of books. I took his left hand, but still felt uncomfortable, wondering if this was meant as an insult.

Holding hands

Men often walk down the street holding a close male friend's hand (right hand with left). Women also do this with other women. Even though the left hand is used, this is not an insult. This happened to me in Lebanon 20 years ago when an Arab friend gently grasped my hand as we walked along. It was a friendly gesture, but it still felt strange. It certainly does not have the same connotation of men holding hands as in the West.

Men and women

Greetings between men and women can be awkward. When I am introduced to a Muslim woman, I am never certain how she will react. Many Muslim women feel they should not physically touch another man who is not their husband or an immediate member of their family. Therefore, I never put out my hand first. If she wants to shake my hand, she will usually reach hers out to me, which tells me it is OK. When I'm unsure, I usually just touch my right hand to my heart and nod slightly to her.

In general, women—especially young women—should not reach out their hands first when being introduced to a Muslim man. If he reaches out his hand first, it is usually OK to shake it back.

An extremely religious Muslim woman might even refuse to shake a non-Muslim woman's hand for fear of becoming ritually unclean. One Pakistani woman would never shake my wife's hand unless hers was first holding a dishrag for "protection."

Of course, none of these greetings is a strict rule. They will vary based on how modern or westernized our Muslim friend is. But when in doubt, it is always better to err on the side of politeness.

"Greet each other with a holy kiss"

When good friends meet, they often embrace and kiss each other on the cheek, often several times in succession (always men with men and women with women). If this happens to you, it's a good sign.

Greeting phrases

When greeting someone—even someone you have met many times before—there are invariably some ritual pleasantries to be exchanged before "getting down to business." These may include phrases such as, "How is your health?" "How is your family?" "How is their health?" A Muslim greeting another Muslim will usually initiate the amenities with "Peace be upon you," which requires the response, "And upon you be peace." A number of my close Muslim friends greet me with these words, and I respond warmly in kind, knowing it is meant as a compliment. I have heard of other Christians who adamantly oppose using these Muslim greetings because they may imply that you are Muslim. I don't agree! All of my friends know I am not a Muslim. And what better greeting is there than, "Peace be upon you"? (Check out Jesus' greeting in John 20:19.)

Refreshments

If you come into a Muslim home or office, you will be greeted with something to drink (usually tea, juice, or a soft drink) and often something to eat (nuts or sweets). Be sure to offer refreshments to your Muslim visitors. If you don't, you may be considered brusque and impolite, confirming the Muslim view that Westerners are cold.

HOSPITALITY AND GENEROSITY

While we lived in Lebanon, my wife and I were invited to the home of one of my students. He and his family lived in a dilapidated Palestinian refugee camp south of Beirut. Although they were poor, they served us on their best dishes and set the largest portions of food before us. Even their friends came by to greet us. In every Muslim home I have visited, this scenario has been repeated. On several such visits, I (or one of my family members) have made the mistake of admiring a household object—a plate or a necklace—only to have that object wrapped up and given to us as a gift on our way out the door.

Hospitality and generosity are two of the most valued attributes in Eastern culture. Every host, no matter how poor, wants to be known as hospitable and generous. A lack of these subtracts from family honor, which is to be avoided at all costs. Generosity is a sign of honor. Be appreciative, but be cautious of what you admire!

When someone visits you, set out nice dishes and serve fruit, nuts, sweets, and tea. Be prepared for a long visit—often several hours—and don't be the first to suggest that the visit is over. (This is usually done by the guest, not the host.) When visiting someone's home for the first time, take along a gift, such as flowers or candy. When you leave, you may be given a container with some of the food that was served. Never return the container empty. Always put something in it, such as sweets or other food that you have made or bought.

GIFTS

In the Eastern world, gifts have greater significance than in the West. **Gifts are *expected* when visiting someone's home for the first time.** It may be small and inexpensive, such as flowers or candy. Gifts are also expected on special occasions or when someone returns from a long trip. The closer your relationship, the more expensive the gift should be.

Bangladeshi friends of mine were in the United States living on graduate support and barely making ends meet. A distant cousin was getting married back home. The family expected this couple to send a monetary gift of at least $500. My friends took out a loan on their credit card to meet this expectation. It would have been too painful to live the rest of their lives hearing about how the "rich relatives living in America" didn't give an appropriate wedding gift.

Try to keep gifts approximately even. A disproportionate gift means that the receiver is under obligation. The student I mentioned earlier, who visited our home with her fiancé, brought an

ornate tea set with stand, cups, saucers, and server. We accepted
the gift but were puzzled by it. From her viewpoint, she had done
me a favor by giving me a nice gift. Later, when I caught her cheating, it was difficult for her to understand why I would not "recip-
rocate" by overlooking her effort to help a friend on the test.

When visiting someone less well off than you, keep your gift
small. Your friend should not have trouble reciprocating at a later
date. Gifts are seen as obligations, and Muslims will do almost
anything not to be in your debt.

FOOD AND DRINK

Muslims believe that God has forbidden them to eat pork or
to drink alcohol. (They assume that Christians do both.) Some
devout Muslims who are invited into your home may be reluctant
to eat or drink anything served on your dishes or cooked with
your utensils for fear that they have been in contact with "unclean"
food. But this is rare; most Muslim guests are only concerned with
actually eating unclean food.

I quietly let any first-time visitors know beforehand that I will
never serve them anything that is unclean or forbidden, and this
is a relief to them. "Safe" foods are usually referred to as *halaal*
(ha-LAAL), or "permitted." Formally, halaal foods have been prepared and blessed in the traditional Islamic way (a Muslim speaks
appropriate words over the animal as it is being slaughtered). My
wife and I once purchased some special halaal chicken from a
local international grocery store, after finding out a guest we had
invited over observed this dietary restriction.

As long as you're not serving pork, almost any other kind of
meat will be fine for the average Muslim you invite to your home.
Chicken is always a safe choice. (Unclean foods also include
any products made with lard and even some gelatin products.
Approximately 5 percent of Jell-O® is made with animal products.) When in doubt, ask your friends if they have special dietary
restrictions.

All you need reasonably do is check the labels on foods you
buy, especially anything prepared with fat (such as cookies or

cakes). Make sure they have been made with vegetable fat and not with lard. Most foods labeled as "kosher" will also be acceptable. The key is to *always check labels* beforehand. This will save you many awkward—even painful—encounters.

DOGS

Throughout most of the Islamic world, dogs are considered dirty animals and are certainly not kept inside the house. Sometimes Muslims have guard dogs, but they are always kept outside. If you have a dog and are trying to relate to Muslims, keep the dog outside. If you must have it inside, keep it restrained, and out of the way and out of sight of your friend during the visit. If the dog rushes up to your friend—as most dogs do—and makes any contact, your guest will probably try to be polite, although he won't be happy about the encounter. He is no longer considered ritually clean and cannot pray again until he performs specific religious cleansing.

CLOTHING

Most Muslims are repelled by the way Westerners dress. I know of one Muslim who, although he was attracted to the Messiah Jesus as a person, could not bring himself to embrace Him as Lord and Savior. He was afraid that by doing so, "the women in my family would have to dress like Western women and become immoral."

Christians visiting another country should follow that culture's standards of modesty in dress. For men, this means wearing long pants (not shorts) and always wearing a shirt, even in summer. The guidelines for women are more strict. In most Muslim countries, women should wear long skirts or dresses and long-sleeved, loose-fitting blouses (definitely nothing sleeveless, and no shorts, low-cut necklines, or two-piece bathing suits). In less restrictive countries, women may wear loose-fitting pants, but the blouse should come down and cover the buttocks. Depending on the country, headscarves and *abayas* (black robes) may be required. If you are in a country in which a headscarf is not required for foreign women, you may want to wear the scarf out of respect anyway. But be careful, as this often communicates that you are a Muslim. If you have any questions about this, ask your host. If you are uncertain, it is always better to err on the side of respect.

What about dress in our country—or even in your own home? Again, modesty and respect are key. It is probably OK for a man to wear shorts, but only around other men. For women, sleeves are essential, and dresses or pants should be below the knee.

MIXED-GENDER MINISTRY

In general, men should minister to men and women to other women. It's especially inappropriate for a single Christian woman to attempt ministry with a Muslim man.

Mixed-gender ministry can confuse the emotions of both parties. Here's a common scenario: If a Christian woman shows attention to a Muslim man, he may get the wrong signals. (Muslim women do not show interest in a man unless they want to pursue a deeper relationship with him.) The Muslim man may be quite charming and know how to court a woman. It is not unusual for the Christian woman to fall in love and marry the man, hoping he will become a believer in Christ. Their children are given Muslim names and are raised as Muslims. For the sake of family peace, the woman may convert to Islam and wear the head covering. You're probably thinking, "That's pretty rare." Not so! One English fellow laborer, who frequently lectures in churches, told me it is rare for him to speak in a church in England whose congregation has not been touched at least once in this way.

So what should single women do? If you find a Muslim man who appears to be interested in the Gospel, get another Christian man involved in the process right away. Why do I present this as one-sided—a Christian woman and a Muslim man? It usually is one-sided. It is rare for a Muslim woman to have, or take, the opportunity to talk privately with a Christian man. Her family and friends would never allow it. But if a Christian man does happen to start sharing with a Muslim woman, he should immediately get another Christian woman involved.

Does this mean there is never a place for mixed-gender ministry? By no means! I have discussed the Gospel with a friend while his wife listened behind a curtain. This happened with a Yemeni family. I asked the husband a spiritual question, and his wife burst from behind the curtain, holding a wooden spoon in her hand, and shouted out the answer.

I have had a Muslim husband ask my wife a spiritual question (with me present, of course) that he was too embarrassed to ask me. Note the key here: This is done in a family/group setting, never one-on-one!

EAST MEETS WEST

Of course, not all Muslims come from traditional backgrounds. In the Middle East, just like in the United States, malls serve as local teen hotspots, and designer jeans, Nike shoes, and portable CD players abound.

I have Muslim friends and acquaintances who run the gamut in adapting to Western culture. Z, a respected professor at an American Midwestern university and a leader at the local mosque, wears a business suit and speaks flawless English. His wife wears traditional Afghani dress, and her face is tattooed with tribal markings. After 20 years in the United States, she speaks almost no English. Their daughter, who graduated from an American high school, now practices medicine across town. Her children are U.S. citizens. The first time I met them, out of politeness I did not reach out my hand to Z's wife, but the physician daughter immediately stretched out hers to shake mine.

M, from Saudi Arabia, loves American slang, drives an SUV, and wears a baseball cap. After graduating in engineering, he dreams of going home to study for a Ph.D. in Islamics.

From tiny villages, tattoos, and traditional dress to satellite dishes, skateboards, and cell phones, Muslims in all countries are being influenced by the Western world. To some extent, every Muslim is a mixture of two cultures. Rather than being a stumbling block, this Eastern-Western mix actually makes it easier for us to relate to Muslims. Understanding our Muslim friends and their Eastern backgrounds demonstrates love and opens the door for potential friendships. But, because we are Westerners, we will most naturally relate to them through our own Western perspective. When Muslim guests visit my home, I feel free to serve American food. I play chess with them. We watch movies. I take them canoeing, to American football games, and to play miniature golf.

BE GENUINE

An Iranian friend once told me the story of his father buying a home. The sales agent said to my friend's father, "I like you." Later in the conversation, the agent again said, "I like you." This happened a third time, and my friend's father suddenly called off the deal. He explained to the agent: "The first time you told me you liked me, I believed you. The second time, I became suspicious. The third time you said it, I knew you were lying to me."

It's uncomfortable when people are overly ingratiating, and it's easy to see through. When you're disingenuous, you're not honoring other people or God. Legitimacy is key. Ask God to provide natural and legitimate opportunities to love and serve others in a Christlike way. **Be yourself with your Muslim friends. Do things with them that are natural for you.** Take them to a sporting event. Bring them home for macaroni and cheese. Watch a video together. Take them on a hike or picnic. Be culturally sensitive, but don't pretend to be something you're not.

GROUP DYNAMICS

Eastern cultures tend to be more group-oriented than Western culture. Most socializing—visits, studying, feasts, and so on—is done in groups. Most of the interacting you do with Muslims will probably take place in a group setting.

Spending time one-on-one also happens, though, and most Muslims will prefer this if they are sharing deep and potentially threatening truths. However, they will only share personal issues with someone they really trust, and this is rare. In the East, anything negative soon finds its way to the ears of friends and family.

The result is shame and a loss of honor. It's easy to see why mutual mistrust is so prevalent in Eastern culture. But there is a positive side to this. I have found that most Muslims living cross-culturally would rather share personal struggles with a Westerner than with another Muslim.

In the West, we are usually free to ask threatening questions without being ostracized. Our whole basis of education centers on the necessity of asking questions and learning to think for ourselves. Education in the Eastern world is based more on rote memory than on integration and application of relevant facts. I saw this many times as a teacher.

This brings up an interesting paradox. In the West, we tend to be long on information but short on social glue. We have the freedom to search and find answers, but we often have no one to share them with. Easterners are just the opposite—long on social glue but short on satisfying answers. Both are essential to our overall witness.

How do you apply this dynamic in ministry? First, learn to value time spent in group situations. Second, pray and look for opportunities to go spiritually deeper with Muslim friends, but *don't do this in group settings!*

When talking with two or more Muslims, they will probably not feel free to share deeply. Instead, they will put on a united front and defend their religious ideals. Anything else could be reported back negatively to others. For example, two Palestinian friends once came to drink tea in my home in New Mexico. I had already spent a lot of time with them both. I asked if they would like to study one of the gospels with me. When they said "no," I was confused. A week later I talked with one of them privately and asked the same question. His answer this time, when he was alone, was "yes."

THE IMPORTANCE OF REPETITION

When I was teaching in Lebanon, I needed a key to my office. I went to the administrator's secretary and politely asked for one. I was told, "Yes," and I left happy. A week passed and there was no key. I asked a second time and again was told, "Yes, it is coming." Another week went by, and still there was no key. Finally, I stomped into the office, pounded my fist on the desk, and said, "I WANT MY KEY!" The secretary looked up and smiled, saying, "Why Dr. Hoskins, you're becoming Lebanese."

Another time, in Saudi Arabia, I showed up for an invitation that was only extended once. My host was relaxing on the sofa when I arrived. Surprised, he tucked his shirt into his pants and scurried around to find something to serve.

In the Middle East, when someone says something only once, it is usually a polite statement or request, but it's not intended to be fulfilled. The person on the receiving end knows this. To a Muslim, repetition intensifies a request.

After returning from Lebanon, my 3-year-old daughter was invited to an American friend's birthday party. She was offered a piece of cake. Knowing she was expected to politely refuse the first offer, she did so. The cake disappeared. My daughter left hungry and disappointed at this "lack of hospitality." How often have our Muslim friends felt that way in our country?

A Muslim's politeness may even shock a Westerner. One day, for example, I walked down the street of Beirut and passed a stranger eating a sandwich. Out of politeness, he held the sandwich up and offered it to me. I was expected to understand this and politely refuse. He would be stunned if I accepted his invitation.

The important thing to remember is that if an offer is genuine, it will be repeated. At that point, you can feel free to either gently refuse or accept. Either way, honor, generosity, and hospitality have all been affirmed, and that's the key in Muslim culture.

When you invite a Muslim to your home, don't be afraid to repeat the invitation so they know they are genuinely wanted.

SAY IT WITH A SMILE

Nonverbal communication, such as body language or tone of voice, often carries more weight than spoken words. This means that when verbal and nonverbal cues don't match up, people tend to believe what is "really" spoken by the nonverbal communication. For example, "good morning" means something entirely different when said sarcastically.

Keep this in mind, especially if you are disagreeing with a Muslim friend. Many Americans tend to look stern, or even frown, when presenting an opposing idea. A dear Lebanese friend gave me a never-forgotten piece of advice: "You can say anything to a Muslim if you say it with a smile on your face."

WORDS GUARANTEED TO START AN ARGUMENT

Certain words or phrases trigger emotional responses, whether we intend for them to or not. Using the wrong word can overshadow anything of importance we hoped to communicate. For example, consider the words "wifely submission" to a feminist, or "evolution" to most evangelical believers, or "absolute truth" to a postmodernist. No matter how we use them, these are loaded terms guaranteed to halt a genuine discussion.

Like us, our Muslim friends react to emotionally loaded words. Here are just a few: church, convert, baptism, cross, crusade, Son of God, Savior, Israel, Jew, Christmas—even the term "Christian" itself. Although I'm not saying, "Don't use these words," I recommend that you be thoughtful, prayerful, and intentional when doing so.

Ask yourself this question: Are there other words—less emotionally charged words—that I could use to get across the same idea? Here are some possibilities:

Use	Instead of
place of worship	church
one who enters the Kingdom	convert
identification with Christ	baptism
means of Roman execution	cross
campaign	crusade
rescuer	Savior
Palestine	Israel
feast of Christ's birth	Christmas
follower of Isa (Jesus)	Christian

I have also found it helpful and appreciated by my friends to refer to Jesus in the Qur'anic way: "Messiah Jesus Son of Mary." There is nothing untrue or disrespectful about this phrase. (See page 55 for a sample of a culturally sensitive testimony.)

DISCUSS, DON'T DEBATE

Most Christians love to debate. Evolution, abortion, the environment, stem-cell research—you name it, we'll debate it. Muslims are equally eager to debate religious topics, such as "Is the Bible the Word of God?" or "Is Jesus the final prophet?"

Add to this scenario a believer's desire to see something positive happen in what is ordinarily a slow ministry, and you've got a recipe for disaster.

Like others, I was excited early on to study apologetics. I wanted to have all my ducks in a row and be ready to debate. I believed that if I could present enough facts, my Muslim friends would admit I was right and come to know Christ. At that time, I was getting to know a Jordanian family who seemed interested in my friendship and spiritual matters as well. They asked what I thought about the gospel of Barnabus, a heretical fourteenth-century forgery on the life of Christ. I had just studied this topic. I was informed and ready to debate. I charged ahead and "won" the debate but wound up nearly destroying the relationship!

It's important to know the basics of Christianity and Islam and to know how they compare and contrast. Having this information will give you confidence and provide answers to Muslims who are genuinely searching. But remember that **it takes time for a friendship to develop to the point at which it can bear the intensity of the Gospel.**

God gifts some to be apologists involved in debating. That's great, but I don't think it's the norm. As for me, when presented with the opportunity to attend or participate in a debate, I avoid it. I tell my friends that I am happy to discuss a topic but not to debate. I tell them that discussions are for friends and debates are for opponents. This gives an opportunity to steer the conversation toward a genuine question they may be asking.

SILENCE IMPLIES AGREEMENT

I have found that Muslims often are more vocal in their beliefs than Christians are. They are more likely to state exactly what they believe, and we are more likely to try to avoid offending them out of politeness. I believe this happens, at least partially, because of cultural differences in communication. In the West, we have a "pause culture." We believe that we should politely wait for a pause in another person's comments before we interject our own thoughts. Obviously, there are many exceptions to this, but generally it is considered rude to interrupt another speaker.

I have found that in the East, people anticipate others' statements and interject without waiting for a pause. In fact, they often think a pause means the other person has nothing important to say—or agrees with what has just been said! Muslims are often amazed at how "wimpy"—uncertain and ashamed of our own beliefs—we Western believers appear to be.

So what should you do if a Muslim friend makes a comment you don't agree with? I usually look for some sort of minimal pause and say something like, "Although I don't agree with what you have just said, I do understand and respect your viewpoint." I make sure to "say it with a smile." If my friend wants to know more, he can ask (and often does). He also does not assume that I agree with him.

MONEY

As closer friendships with Muslims develop, it is common for them to ask for money when they have needs. In their culture, a true friend is expected to help if he can. Yet the Scriptures warn us to avoid unnecessary financial entanglements because they lead to difficult obligatory relationships (owing—Romans 13:8; borrowing—Proverbs 22:7; cosigning—Proverbs 6:1).

Every time I have loaned money to a friend, it has backfired, significantly straining the relationship. One Muslim friend asked me to cosign for a small loan ($400) he was applying for. I showed him the passage in Proverbs that commands us not to cosign for loans. My friend left disappointed and confused. In retrospect, after explaining about cosigning, I should have offered him the money as a gift. My advice is to avoid loans whenever possible. If a person has a genuine financial need, offer the money as a gift if you're able. He can repay it later if he wishes. However, make it clear that you consider him under no obligation to pay you back. Finally, don't expect to see the money again, and don't ask for it. If the amount is too large, honestly tell him that you don't loan money (or cosign for loans) and that you don't have enough to give it as a gift. This is uncomfortable any time it comes up. Be sure to pray and ask for God's wisdom to help you find a creative alternative to just saying "No."

TALKING POLITICS

On a trip to Lebanon, we watched from our balcony as Israeli jets bombed the power facilities located within a few football fields of our residence. For Americans watching at home, it meant a 15-second segment on CNN sandwiched between sports scores and beer commercials. For those living in the midst of it, it meant fear, frustration, and anger—in that order. Similar scenarios are constantly being played out in many other countries around the world.

When talking with Easterners, you'll probably hear comments like these:

> *"If America wanted peace in the Middle East, they could make it happen in 24 hours."*
> *"Why does the United States unilaterally support Israel against the Arabs?"*
> *"All the problems in the Middle East are the fault of the United States."*
> *"They don't care about us. All they care about is oil."*

Whether or not these assertions are true is not the point. What is important is that the overwhelming majority of Muslims—in the United States and abroad—believe they are true. What's more, these perceptions have erected significant barriers to befriending and sharing the Gospel with Muslims. So how should we respond?

First, I think we should sympathetically listen without arguing either for or against their assertions. Second, be learners. Take time to read and study the issues. I have included several resources in the suggested reading list; especially note the books by Elias Chacour and Christine Mallouhi. Third, look for opportunities to steer the conversation onto spiritual ground. (Note how Jesus did this in Luke 13:1–9.) Fourth, the Lord may give you the opportunity to be a practical and positive force for justice in our own governmental system through letter writing or personal contacts.

Finally, pray that God would use these topics to open your friends' hearts to the truth of the Gospel. And let's ask God to give *us* a more balanced view of what is going on in the world around us.

PERSONAL SAFETY

Until recently, life for most Americans seemed relatively safe. The events of September 11, 2001, changed that. We can no longer live in oblivion to the tension between Muslims and non-Muslims, especially Western non-Muslims. We may feel the effects corporately (as a nation) or even personally.

Several years ago, the night before I was to leave on a trip to the Middle East, a Muslim friend phoned me with a warning. "Dr. Hoskins, be very careful. I overheard some students talking. They called their own government to tell them that you were coming to bring Christianity to them." When I discussed this with another Middle Eastern friend living in the United States, he told me he was amazed how naïve we Americans are in security matters.

Although ultimately our safety—and that of our Middle Eastern Christian friends—rests in the hands of God, it's our responsibility to take some precautions ourselves. The most important is to **avoid casual name-dropping, both in front of a group or in print. This is especially important if a Muslim comes into a personal relationship with Christ, even in America.** When this happens, our natural response is excitement.

We want to broadcast the news and have the person share his or her testimony in church. But when the local Islamic community gets word of this, it could cost the person dearly.

It's also wise to avoid mentioning Christian organizations and/or laborers who are reaching out to Muslims (either here or abroad). A close friend and fellow laborer was applying for a visa from the embassy of a sensitive Middle Eastern country. The embassy official reached into a file and pulled out a copy of one of this man's recent prayer letters. He was able to get his visa, but he knew he was being closely watched.

Another friend and laborer lived in a different Middle Eastern country. A Christian wrote a book in which this man's name was mentioned. Security officials paid him a visit, and within 10 days he was expelled from the country.

I share these examples not to generate fear, but to help each of us become wiser and more sensitive.

FOLK ISLAM AND SPIRITUAL WARFARE

If you spend much time with Easterners, at some point, you will probably encounter some type of folk Islam. Z was a friend of mine whose father was a demon-controller. He would go to caves and spend weeks at a time "commanding" the *jinn*. (Jinn is the Arabic word for evil spirits, and from it we get our English word "genie.") One of Z's earliest memories is sitting at dinner with an extra place set for the family demon.

The "Hand of Fatima" hangs from the rearview mirror of many cars in the Middle East. This is for good luck and protection from the jinn. Wearing a blue stone is supposed to protect the wearer from the "evil eye."

These are all examples of folk Islam, which orthodox Muslims are opposed to. They believe there is only one true God who demands complete submission. Anything else is idolatry. Still, the impact of folk Islam is extensive, especially on Muslim women. Some laborers estimate that up to 75 percent of Muslims worldwide are significantly influenced by folk Islam. My own experience confirms this.

Folk Islam may well be the natural extension of not being able to have a personal relationship with God. If people do not or cannot know God personally, they will be fearful and will feel the need to try to control their own destiny. This is the essence of folk Islam, and it can be a powerful weapon of the Enemy.

A common misconception among Christians is that *if* demon possession actually exists, it certainly cannot involve us. We see this as a "volume" issue: If we're *filled* with the Spirit, how can there be *room* for anything evil? But the issue is not volume or physical dwelling, but rather one of influence. Followers of Christ can be influenced by Satan.

What is Satan's primary means of influencing us? Jesus described him as "a liar and the father of lies" (John 8:44). Satan's only legitimate source of power over us is the *lies* he tells us that *we believe and then act on*. So how do we counteract this? Jesus said, "You will know the *truth,* and the *truth* will set you free" (John 8:32, emphasis added). Later, Jesus said to Pilate, "For this reason I was born, and for this I came into the world, to testify to the *truth*. Everyone on the side of *truth* listens to me" (John 18:37, emphasis added).

The primary issue in spiritual warfare is truth versus lies. So how can we protect ourselves against Satan's lies? First, we should ask God to show us any lies we may have believed: "Search me, O God, and know my heart; test me and know my anxious thoughts" (Psalm 139:23). The next step is to reject these lies in prayer and claim the truth, which is our rightful heritage. (*The Bondage Breaker* by Neil Anderson is a helpful book on this topic; see the suggested reading list.)

One final—and very important—word of caution: When dealing with folk Islam, you may encounter a person who appears to be under direct demonic control. In these cases, I recommend that you ask God to provide another Christian with experience and gifting in this area to help. I do not recommend directly confronting demonic forces. This may seem exciting, but it can become physically and spiritually dangerous. Find someone with experience in these matters to help you.

THE POWER OF LOVE

In one restricted Middle Eastern country, I was given instructions *not* to do many things. These included being out on the streets during Muslim times of prayer, traveling without a travel pass, drinking or eating openly during Ramadan, allowing my wife and daughter in public without headscarves and abayas, possessing Christian literature and Bibles, worshiping with other Christians, and even wishing others "Merry Christmas." I became discouraged thinking about all the things that were against the local laws. But as I reflected, I was encouraged by the truth in Galatians 5:22–23:

> "But the fruit of the Spirit is love, joy, peace, patience, kindness, goodness, faithfulness, gentleness and self-control. Against such things **there is no law**" (emphasis added).

I thought, "Wow! Look at all the things I *can* do!"

This reminded me of the story of a missionary living in Africa who struggled with learning the local language. One African described him this way: "He doesn't speak our language, but, oh, does he love us!"

It's important to do your homework and know a lot about Islam and the Muslim culture. However, it is far more important to show genuine love—not to successfully accomplish your project, but for the sake of the people you're involved with.

One of my friendships began with a Muslim man in the 105-degree heat of a New Mexico summer. His air conditioner went out, and he called me for help. While he stayed inside with his pregnant wife, I climbed on his roof and fixed a hose that had come loose. Out of gratitude, did he and his entire household surrender their lives to Jesus? Nope! But I did develop a friendship and was able to clearly share the Gospel. I helped him for the sake of Jesus (Matthew 25:40). Period.

We love others only "because he first loved us" (1 John 4:19). There may be no stronger Gospel message than the love we demonstrate, tangibly, to others. We may have mastered our methods, but if we have not love, we are nothing (1 Corinthians 13:2).

EMERGENCY APOLOGETICS
Answering Common Objections

WHEN A MUSLIM MEETS A CHRISTIAN for the first time, invariably he asks questions and raises objections to the Christian faith. His forthright manner may seem rude to a Westerner not used to this style of relating. The Christian may feel threatened and uncomfortable, and usually responds by attempting to present a thorough and logical defense of the Gospel. Either a strident exchange ensues and offends both people, or the Christian, frustrated at not being able to finish his argument, becomes subdued. The Muslim then wonders about the Christian's passivity and lack of courage. This does not bode well for a budding friendship!

There is another option. I have developed some concise responses to a Muslim's common questions about Christianity. They can all be said with a smile and will satisfy most inquirers. Listen carefully to the Muslim's response. It will tell you a lot about his level of spiritual interest. **A Muslim's questions may not be what they appear. He may be searching for more than just your beliefs; he may be probing to find out if you respect him and the views he holds.**

The responses that follow are not intended to be exhaustive apologetics. (See the suggested reading list for other sources.) Rather, they are a way to show that you care about the person and his or her religion and that you're interested in future dialogue.

"THE BIBLE HAS BEEN CORRUPTED."
When Christians hear this, we may be offended and think, "How

35

dare they insult the living, breathing, and eternal Word of God?" Instead of battling, try a different line of reasoning.

Response: "Do you believe that Allah is all powerful? Of course you do! Then isn't He powerful enough to protect His own Word? Of course He is! There is no way that Allah would allow His Word to be changed. No, the Bible has not been corrupted." (Don't forget to smile!) Note that this response is not based on a logical sequence of events, details, and exposition. It is focused on God's character.

"CHRISTIANS BELIEVE IN THREE GODS."

When Muslims say this, they are referring to statements appearing in the Qur'an and *ahadith* (traditions) based on misunderstandings and early church heresies prevalent at the time of Muhammad. For example, they mistakenly believe that "trinity" means God, Mary, and Jesus.

Response: "Christians also believe there is only one God. In the Old Testament of the Bible, we find one of God's most significant statements to His people: 'The LORD our God, the LORD is one' (Deuteronomy 6:4). No, Christians do not believe in three gods."

I often add that Christians do believe God can appear functionally in different forms. For example, God appeared to Moses in the form of a burning bush. (This is also in the Qur'an.) We believe that God has a spirit (His living essence) and a word (His spoken personality) who took the form of a man, Messiah Jesus. In the Qur'an, Jesus is also known as God's Spirit and God's Word.

"JESUS IS NOT THE SON OF GOD."

Many Muslims think that Christians believe God had sexual intercourse with Mary, and Jesus was the physical result. Of course, Christians do not believe that at all.

Response: "The term 'son' shows deep respect, relationship, and intimacy. In the Bible, Jesus is known by many terms: 'Son of David,' 'Son of Man,' as well as 'Son of God.' None implies physical sonship resulting from the sexual union of a man and woman. In the Qur'an, a term is used for a wanderer or wayfarer on a jour-

36

ney, called *Ibn Sabeel* (Ibn-sa-BEEL), or Son of the Road. Does this mean that two roads had sexual intercourse, which physically resulted in another road? Of course not! In the same way, when Jesus is called the Son of God, it is a respectful term implying an intimate relationship."

"WHAT DO YOU THINK ABOUT MUHAMMAD?"

To a Muslim, Muhammad is the most precious person in the world. How you respond to this question will set the tone for any future relationship. **Be honest, but refer to Muhammad with respect, just as you would want your Muslim friend to be respectful of Jesus.**

Response: "You know that Muhammad is not my prophet; he is yours. Although I do not believe exactly what you believe about him, I do respect him. Politically, he was a reformer, a statesman, and a national leader. Religiously, he called idolatrous people back to worship the one true God. He also said many positive things about my Lord Jesus. I believe each of these reasons makes him worthy of my respect."

"WHAT DO YOU THINK ABOUT THE QUR'AN?"

Response: "As a Christian, you know that the Qur'an is not my book; it is yours. Although I don't believe exactly what you believe about the Qur'an, I do read it. I appreciate it because of the many wonderful and beautiful things it says about my Lord Messiah Jesus."

"WHY HAVEN'T YOU BECOME A MUSLIM?"

Response: "You know that I'm a Christian, which means I'm not a follower of your religion, your prophet, or your book. However, if you are using the word 'Muslim' ('surrendered') in its truest sense—as one who is surrendered to God—then I am already that. I have surrendered my life to God and have been made completely clean through His mighty blood sacrifice of Messiah Jesus."

"WAS MUHAMMAD PROPHESIED IN THE BIBLE?"

Muslims believe the Bible prophesies the coming of Muhammad, beginning with the call of Abraham (Genesis 12:1–3):

> *"The LORD had said to Abram, 'Leave your country, your people and your father's household and go to the land I will show you. I will make you into a great nation and I will bless you; I will make your name great, and you will be a blessing. I will bless those who bless you, and whoever curses you I will curse; and all peoples on earth will be blessed through you.'"*

Muslims believe this worldwide blessing is the arrival of Islam. They interpret this to mean that God will make a great nation through Hagar and her son Ishmael (Genesis 17:20).

They also believe Moses prophesied about Muhammad in Deuteronomy 18:18:

> *"I will raise up for them a prophet like you from among their brothers; I will put my words in his mouth, and he will tell them everything I command him."*

Response: "I do believe that God, in the Bible, prophesied about a very special prophet who would come in the future. A few of the prophecies could be confused with Muhammad. However, there are more than 300 prophecies, which are very specific. As I have studied them, I believe there is only one person who could (and did) fulfill each of them—the Messiah Jesus, Son of Mary. Sometime, would you like to look at a few of these prophecies?" Gently, and with a smile, point the way back to Jesus and the Scriptures.

Without compromising the truth, respond to these common objections and others like them with short, concise, and respectful answers. **Our goal is not to win an argument but to gain a friend and a hearing for the Gospel.**

CHAPTER 5

SIX KEYS
TO COMMUNICATING
THE GOSPEL

FROM PERSONAL OBSERVATION and the experiences of others, I have found that Muslims making their journey toward the Kingdom require six things:
1. Prayer by the saints
2. Friendship with at least one genuine Christian
3. Culturally relevant application from the Bible
4. Bridges built through Muslim culture
5. The "wooing" of the Spirit, without which nothing else matters
6. The insider approach

PRAYER
The Bible commands Jesus' followers to be alert, devoted to prayer, and to pray continually: for laborers for the harvest field (Matthew 9:37–38), for opportunities to share the Gospel (Colossians 4:2–3), and for the salvation of those outside the Kingdom (Romans 10:1). In some mysterious way, prayer binds us together with the heart and mind of God, allowing us to participate with Him as He creates new life in Christ.

As you pray for your Muslim friends, consider the following prayers based on passages from Scripture: 1) that God would draw them near to Him (John 6:44); 2) that their hearts will be good soil for the Gospel (Luke 8:15); 3) that they will hear the Gospel and listen (Acts 28:28); and 4) that God will raise up indigenous laborers among Muslim people (Matthew 9:36–38).

If you need other ideas for ways to pray, consider these:

Fasting

Fasting can be as simple as praying while skipping a single meal or abstaining from a certain food item. When facing a particularly thorny spiritual issue, you may feel led to fast more extensively, such as going two or three days, or even longer, without food. Before considering anything more than a partial fast, I recommend that you read Arthur Wallis's book *God's Chosen Fast* (see the suggested reading list) and consult with your family doctor.

There is nothing magical about fasting. However, it does remove distractions and keep us focused on prayer. It also shows God that we are serious.

Prayer walking

For more than five years, a friend of mine has performed a weekly prayer walk around a local mosque, praying for individuals and situations. During the walk, my friend uses different acronyms to help, such as praying through the letters of the alphabet to voice praises to the Lord (A—Almighty; B—Beneficent; C—Comforter, etc.).

Praying for crisis

A mentor and fellow laborer gave me this prayer idea: asking God to bring about crisis situations in friends' lives. This also means that we need to be available to help them through the crisis. This is asking, "Lord, please do whatever is necessary to get my friend's attention." Note, however, that crisis-situation prayers should be Spirit-inspired and never done thoughtlessly or rashly.

Praying with them

In addition to praying *for* my Muslim friends, I try to pray *with* them when possible and appropriate. Note that it will seldom *feel* appropriate. The key here is not to be timid but to boldly ask and see what the Lord does. After visiting friends in the hospital, I ask if I may pray aloud for them in Jesus' name. I have never been refused. My Muslim friends have always been grateful and touched by this gesture.

Praying with other believers

Finally, it is crucial to recruit other believers to partner with you in prayer. Give them specific names and requests. Ask God to surround you with people who are gifted prayer warriors.

DEVELOPING FRIENDSHIPS

Compared to our Western relationships, friendships with Muslims take longer to develop, and trust is given more slowly. Once it is given, however, it usually lasts longer and goes deeper. Building these types of friendships requires significant commitment. Here are some essentials in making that happen.

Open up

We must open ourselves up, being willing to love and be loved in return. This takes effort and is often inconvenient. We must also be willing to open up our time and our circles. Through hospitality, common interests, and being available to people in crisis, we open ourselves to others.

Become a learner

According to Webster's Dictionary, "communication" is both the giving and receiving of information. Many Westerners get caught up in the "giving/teaching" part and neglect the receiving aspect of communication. A mentor of mine stated that if we desire to be used by God in the Muslim world, we must learn to operate out of a "receiving" mode. We must commit ourselves to becoming learners rather than teachers. This really shouldn't be too difficult—our Muslim friends are our navigators as we seek to explore their cultural waters. The most profound lessons I have learned have come from my Muslim friends.

Be legitimate

Ask God for friendships that are legitimate—from our friends' perspective as well as our own. For an ongoing relationship to be successful, our Muslim friends must be able to explain to their family and friends why they continue to meet with us. If it does not appear to be legitimate, family and close friends may discourage your friend from continuing the relationship. The next thing you know, your friend will be avoiding you.

Focus on the long term
Finally, we must look at friendships from a long-term perspective. This is more difficult for us in the West who develop trust quicker but tend to be more superficial. Our friendships often last only as long as we are in close proximity. Not so in the East. Deep friendships in the Eastern world are lifelong. It is common to receive letters, e-mails, phone calls, and even spontaneous visits long after friends have moved apart.

MAKING THE BIBLE CULTURALLY RELEVANT
"Consequently, faith comes from hearing the message, and the message is heard through the word of Christ" (Romans 10:17).

We may have wonderful friendships with Muslims, but for the Holy Spirit to spark new life, exposure to God's Word is required. This is the fun part, and it's not nearly as difficult as people think. I have found question-asking to be the most helpful initial technique, followed by telling stories and using analogies. All of these may lead to serious Bible reading and/or study. In everything, focus on the Kingdom of God. That's what Jesus did (Matthew 5–7; 13; 18; 20–22).

Ask questions
Begin developing a list of questions and try them out with your Muslim friends. These should be open-ended (not answerable with a simple "yes" or "no"), focus on eternal issues, and turn the conversation to Jesus and the Scriptures. Consider questions like these:
1. What makes a person "clean" or "unclean" in Islam?
2. I understand that animal sacrifices are important in Islamic

culture. When the animal is sacrificed, what deeper meaning does this have?

3. What is the difference between "sin" and being "unclean" in Islam?
4. How is sin removed from a person in Islam?
5. What are the things we can learn about God's eternal Kingdom from man's temporal kingdoms?
6. In Islam, how can people know for certain that God will allow them to enter paradise on the Day of Judgment?
7. In Islam, what is the significance of a person's dreams?
8. In Islam, what things are considered honorable (or shameful)?
9. There are many prophets that overlap in both Islam and Christianity (Adam, Noah, Solomon, Jonah, and others). According to Islam, what were the primary messages of these prophets?
10. Jesus is known as the Messiah in both Islam and Christianity. Why do you think He has this title? What do you think it means?

You can follow up these questions by sharing a relevant passage or story from the Bible. They may even want to read it with you.

Remain alert for genuine questions from your friends, and play off of these to form your own questions. Finally, pray that God will give you discernment to look for the best question in any given circumstance.

Use stories

Everyone loves stories. Notice how the audience perks up when a story comes along during a sermon or speech. Jesus regularly used stories to communicate with His audience. Depending on your own style and opportunities, Jesus' stories may be read and studied together with a friend.

Another powerful tool is sharing personal faith stories. When talking with an Indonesian woman, my wife related a story from early in our marriage. We were out of money and prayed to God, in Jesus' name, for help. At the last minute, the exact amount of money we needed came through. The woman got excited and said, "I want to hear more stories like that one!" (Here's a pearl to tuck away: **Our friends always love to hear about answers to prayer. Whenever you experience this, share it with your friends.**)

Arguably the most powerful faith story is your own personal testimony—the story of how you came to know Christ. Take time to write out your testimony, then rework it. Look for emotionally loaded terms that may not relate—and worse, may inflame. (For an example of my own testimony, modified for cultural sensitivity, see page 55.) Practice giving your testimony. If you don't feel particularly adept at sharing it verbally, write it down and hand it out to friends on an individual basis.

Use analogies
The best kind of teaching usually begins by building on something that a person already knows. Analogies use something concrete from a Muslim's culture to illustrate what Jesus did for us on the cross. Here are some ideas:

1. Cultural ideals
While visiting with some Pakistani friends, I asked, "What would happen in your culture if you accidentally killed someone and then were caught by the injured family?" I was told that you would have to be killed. I then asked what the ideal solution for that situation would be. I was told, "Of course it would be best to be generous and forgive that person."

"But would that ever take place?" I asked. My friend said, "No, never." The door was open for further discussion, such as the topics of "payment for crimes" and atonement.

2. Cleanliness/Uncleanliness
We were invited by fellow laborers to meet their Lebanese friends. They had been unable to generate meaningful spiritual conversations and wanted some advice. While drinking tea with the Lebanese family, I asked them, "What specific things make a

person clean or unclean in Islam?" The father's eyes lit up like someone had turned on his power supply. He went into a half-hour monologue on Islamic regulations. Our laborer friends were amazed at the breakthrough. And the door was open for multiple entry points to the Gospel ("That reminds me of a story that Messiah Jesus told . . . " or "The Torah of our Bible speaks about that when it says . . . ").

3. Concept of sacrifice

A common new year's banner seen throughout the Middle East is translated, "May each year be good to you." The banner carries a picture of a lamb or sheep. In Lebanon, when a new movie theater opened, a sheep would be sacrificed in front for good luck. This also happens for special celebrations, such as *Eid Al Ad-ha* (EED Al- AD-ha), the Feast of the Sacrifice. When I've asked what this means, most Muslims tell me they don't know. Others say it is just for good luck. Some think that it has some connection to the story in the Qur'an in which Abraham was commanded by Allah to sacrifice his only son, Ishmael. (The Qur'an does not actually say it was Ishmael, but Islamic tradition teaches this.) This can lead to a fruitful discussion.

4. Stories common to the Bible and Qur'an

It is encouraging to think about the many areas Christians have in common with Muslims. To be sure, we have many differences, and we would be foolish not to acknowledge them. But let's begin where our Muslim friends *are,* rather than where they are not. Many stories and people are common to the Bible and Qur'an: Creation, Adam and Eve, the Fall, Noah and the Flood, Abraham, Isaac, Ishmael, David and Goliath, Solomon, Jonah, Jesus, and others. These can be used to illustrate redemption and faith.

Bible reading and study

This is the evangelistic method Western Christians are most familiar with: simply reading or studying Bible topics or passages with your friend. Using questions to study the Bible is helpful:

"What does it say?" (content), "What does it mean?" (interpretation), and "What does it mean to me?" (application).

BUILDING BRIDGES THROUGH MUSLIM CULTURE

"To the weak I became weak, to win the weak. I have become all things to all men so that by all possible means I might save some. I do all this for the sake of the gospel, that I may share in its blessings" (1 Corinthians 9:22–23).

If you want a permanent river crossing, you must have a bridge. We have been commanded by the Lord to take the Gospel to the lost. We have to go to them. God demonstrated this first when He came to us! In the passage above, Paul is talking about building bridges for the Gospel.

Three natural bridges, near and dear to the hearts of all Muslims, already exist: their holy book, the Qur'an; the sayings of their prophet Muhammad contained in their traditions; and their proverbs.

The Qur'an as a bridge

You may wonder whether it's wise to use the Qur'an as a bridge to the Gospel. By doing this, aren't we giving too much credence to the Qur'an? Christians have debated this repeatedly.

My answer is that **the Qur'an should be important to us because it's important to our Muslim friends.** We should not be afraid to compare the Qur'an to the Bible or to use it to illustrate truth.

> " 'The prophet who has a dream [may relate] his dream, but let the one who has my word speak it faithfully. For what has straw to do with grain?' declares the LORD. 'Is not my word like fire,' declares the LORD, 'and like a hammer that breaks a rock in pieces?' " (Jeremiah 23:28–29).

I believe everyone seeking to share their faith with Muslims should have at least a basic familiarity with the Qur'an. This will be helpful as you minister to those who are actively and genuinely searching for the truth.

When Muslims ask for my opinions on the Qur'an, I say, "I am an expert on my book, the Bible, and I am happy to discuss from that perspective. But the Qur'an is your book, and you are the expert, not me." My friends appreciate sensitivity and respect, just as I would if we were talking about the Bible.

(One important point you should be aware of: Muslims do not believe that the Qur'an can be translated. Because it was given originally in Arabic, this is the only form that actually *is* the Qur'an. All other translations give only the "meaning.")

The most helpful Gospel bridges seem to be passages from the Qur'an that contain a direct reference to Jesus. I include a few of these passages below; the applications I leave to you.

Abraham's sacrificing his son: 37 (Al-Safat – The Rangers): 107 "And We ransomed him with a mighty sacrifice." (I have used this with my friends as a picture of Jesus.)

God made Mary and Jesus "a sign for all peoples": 21 (Al-Anbiyaa – The Prophets): 91 "And she who guarded her virginity, so We breathed into her of Our spirit and appointed her and her son to be a sign unto all beings."

Jesus honored and called the Messiah and God's Word: 3 (Aal Imran – House of Imran): 45 When the angels said, "Mary, God gives thee good tidings of a Word from Him whose name is Messiah, Jesus, son of Mary; high honored shall he be in this world and the next, near stationed to God."

Jesus' birth, death, and resurrection: 19 (Maryam – Mary): 33 "Peace be upon me, the day I was born, and the day I die, and the day I am raised up alive!"

Jesus called God's Word and His Spirit: 4: (Al-Nisa – The Women): 171 "The Messiah, Jesus son of Mary, was only the Messenger of God, and His Word that He committed to Mary, and a Spirit from Him."

The traditions as a bridge

Once when I was drinking tea with some Iraqi friends, the conversation turned to the number of cups a guest needed to drink to be polite. The answer was an odd number, either one or three, but not two or four. I mentioned to my friends I believed this came from their oral traditions (*hadith*, singular; *ahadith*, plural). Although the wife did not think this was possible, her husband confirmed my theory.

In my experience, the majority of what most Muslims believe and practice does not come from the Qur'an, as is usually supposed. Rather, it comes from oral traditions, which are a record of Muhammad's words and deeds. These oral traditions are passed on through religious leaders, families, and friends. The goal of many Muslims is to perfectly follow these traditions in every aspect of their lives. It follows, then, that learning about these oral traditions will help us better relate to our Muslim friends.

The oral traditions began being collected from the third to the ninth centuries after Muhammad's death. Probably the most authentic and well-respected collector was Al-Bukhari, who was born in A.D. 811 and died at age 65. He is reputed to have personally collected 300,000 traditions and memorized 200,000. Of these, he thoroughly researched and authenticated 7,068 and compiled these in 93 books of nine volumes. I have yet to meet a Muslim who did not accept the works of Al-Bukhari as authentic. The topics cover a broad range: personal hygiene, marital and women's issues, marriage, birth, death, miracles, fasting, prayer, heaven, hell, *jihad*, and many others. See the suggested reading list for an excellent book by Phil Parshall (*Inside the Community*, Baker Book House) to begin learning about the traditions. A complete copy of Al-Bukhari's traditions (in Arabic with English translations) may be purchased online from Amazon.com and is included in the suggested reading list (by Muhammad M. Khan).

To give you the flavor of the oral traditions, I include one complete tradition. This is my favorite because it illustrates a heart that hungers for a personal God. The English translation from the Arabic is my own and was checked by a native Arabic speaker.

Each tradition begins with a chain of people who transmitted the saying. This chain usually goes back to Muhammad himself or to one who knew him. I include the chain for completeness and to preserve the original style of Al-Bukhari.

Volume 6: Book 60: Number 485: Page 457
Ahmad bin Dauud Abu-Jaafar Al-Munaadi told us that Rowh was told from Saeed bin Abu-Aruba from Qatada from Anis bin Malik that,

The prophet of Allah (peace be unto him) said to Ubai bin Kaab that, "Allah commanded me to recite the Qur'an to you." He said, "Did Allah name me personally to you?" He said, "Yes." He said, "Have I been mentioned by the Lord of the worlds?" He said, "Yes." His eyes flowed (with tears).

Muslim proverbs as a bridge

Muslim proverbs are another effective way to connect Muslims to the truths of the Bible. The late Dr. Samuel Zwemer, a pioneer Christian missionary to Muslims in North Africa and the Middle East during the early twentieth century, was asked what he would do differently, if anything, in evangelizing Muslims. He replied that he would have spent more time studying national proverbs, because this was an important key to the hearts of Muslim people. I have enjoyed studying, memorizing, and using Arabic proverbs in conversation. When a familiar proverb is used, emotions are touched. Sometimes the proverbs can be directly linked to biblical truth. Other times, they are simply a means for better understanding. In either case, they are worthwhile. (See the suggested reading list for more on this.)

THE "WOOING" OF THE SPIRIT

Although the other factors mentioned in this chapter are important, there is a truly magical awakening of a person's spirit that only God can perform. God has chosen, forgiven, and redeemed us (Ephesians 1:3–14), and even our ability to respond must be awakened by Him. Because this is beyond our human understanding, I can only encourage you to pray as Paul did in Ephesians 1:18: "I pray also that the eyes of your heart may be enlightened in order that you may know the hope to which he has called you, the riches of his glorious inheritance in the saints."

THE INSIDER APPROACH

I pray that you will get to see it happen, that the Spirit of God will "woo" your Muslim friend to place his or her trust in Jesus and enter the Kingdom. At this point, you will become a spiritual mentor to your friend, who will probably ask some hard questions about where they go from here.

> "From one man he made every nation of men, that they should inhabit the whole earth; and **he determined the times set for them and the exact places where they should live.** God did this so that men would seek him and perhaps reach out for him and find him, though he is not far from each one of us" (Acts 17:26–27, emphasis added).

In His sovereignty, God perfectly placed every person and people group with the express purpose that they might search for Him and find Him.

> "Nevertheless, **each one should retain the place in life that the Lord assigned to him** and to which God has called him. This is the rule I lay down in all the churches. . . . **Each one should remain in the situation which he was in when God called him.** Were you a slave when you were called? Don't let it trouble you—although if you can gain your freedom, do so. For he who was a slave when he was called by the Lord is the Lord's freedman; similarly, he who was a free man when he was called is Christ's slave. You were bought at a price; do not become slaves of men. Brothers, each man, as responsible to God, should **remain**

in the situation God called him to" *(1 Corinthians 7:17, 20–24, emphasis added).*

Where we are and who we are as we enter God's Kingdom have not been left to chance. They are part of His design. In spite of the injunction to *"remain in the situation,"* I am amazed how quick we are to get a new believer to leave his or her customs, culture, and family traditions to take on the trappings of Western Christianity.

Should we encourage Muslim-background believers to abandon their Islamic customs, culture, family, and values and be immediately baptized so they can become just like us? (Note that in Islamic culture, baptism is the ultimate act of betrayal, symbolizing that a person has left Islam, family, and friends.) Conversely, should we tell all new believers they cannot be baptized or attend church, even if they want to?

I don't believe it is wise to push a new believer toward either extreme. This is a job for the Holy Spirit. Our responsibility is to help a new believer (regardless of background) grow deeper in relationship with Christ and let the Holy Spirit serve as teacher, counselor, comforter, and guide. **Our job is also to make sure our friend knows of the options to stay or leave Islamic culture as the Holy Spirit leads.**

I prayed with a Palestinian man who had surrendered his life to Christ. This young man loves Jesus dearly. He chose to stay within his Islamic community. He wanted other Muslims where he lived and worked to see the love of Christ and the light of the Gospel. He has followed this difficult path for more than 20 years!

I have met a number of Muslim-background believers who consider themselves "truly Muslim," that is, genuinely "surrendered" to God, trusting Him for their salvation, while continuing to live in the Islamic community. I have met others who now openly identify themselves as Christians and have left their Islamic roots. Both groups are being used by God in the ways He intends for them. There is room at His table for both!

FINAL COMMENTS

SOONER OR LATER, ANYONE INVOLVED with ministry to Muslims is faced with a discouraging fact. If Muslims are not the world's most resistant group to the Gospel, then they are certainly in top contention. Missiologists have assigned varying degrees of difficulty in cross-cultural evangelism. Any of the following four characteristics makes the task more difficult. The first characteristic is that of being culturally far from us as opposed to culturally near (Asians vs. Europeans). The second is socioeconomic depression, such as that seen in developing nations. The third is political instability. The fourth characteristic is that of being religiously hostile as opposed to being neutral or supportive. Most Muslim people groups fit into all four of these categories! The uniformly disappointing ministry results we've seen in the past 1,400 years testify to this.

So what keeps us going? To be frank, it's usually not an overwhelming love for the people. Although love is essential, Muslims often seem difficult to love. (This may be a reflection of what was foretold of the children of Ishmael in Genesis 16:11–12.) Neither is it the fast results or the ease of ministry. In my experience, **the single most important factor in persevering on this challenging mission field is the call of God and His commands in Scripture.**

God has promised that one day there will be people from every tribe and tongue and people and nation who will be part of His eternal Kingdom (Revelation 5:9). A similar promise in Isaiah 60:6–7 lists specific tribes: Midian, Ephah, Sheba, Kedar, and Nebaioth. All of these are associated with the Middle East and Arabian Peninsula; Nebaioth and Kedar are listed as the first two sons of Ishmael (Genesis 25:12–13). The promise is that, one day, "they will go up with acceptance" on God's altar.

So what is our responsibility in seeing this promise come about? This is encouraging! Jesus said, "No one can come to me unless the Father who sent me draws him, and I will raise him up at the last day" (John 6:44). What an incredible statement! There is no possible way that any person can come to know Jesus unless God first draws him or her to Himself.

Do we have an active part in living out and proclaiming the Gospel to Muslims? Yes, absolutely. This is clearly commanded (Matthew 28:19–20). Does He want us to pray? Yes, this is also commanded (Colossians 4:2–4). Do we know ahead of time who God has been drawing to Himself? No, that's not for us to know. Our job is to pray, prepare, and proclaim the Gospel and to trust Him to guide us along the way.

Does it depend on how slick our presentation is or how fervently we can debate? Absolutely not, although it is important to be a good steward of the gifts and abilities He has provided. I recall teaching a young believer, Dave, to share his faith in a college dormitory using a tool known as "The Bridge Illustration." Dave was nervous and drew the illustration all wrong. He put God in the wrong place, and even the cross was upside-down. Finally, Dave asked his friend if he wanted to pray to receive Christ as Lord and Savior. That was about the only part he got right. Yet the young man had been prepared by the Holy Spirit, and he prayed right there to receive Christ. I was flabbergasted. Does this mean it's OK to be sloppy in our preparation? Of course not. But it does mean that God, in His sovereignty and grace, covers for a lot of our inadequacy.

You can keep persevering in your witness to Muslims because of the confidence God gives that *the job is not up to you.* God already knows who will come to Him, and He has been preparing genuine seekers to hear the message and respond to Jesus. This is the sovereignty of God. What a privilege He has given us to participate with Him in His work!

CULTURALLY SENSITIVE PERSONAL TESTIMONY

By Ed Hoskins

MY GRANDFATHER WAS A WESTERN COWBOY. From him I learned to love the wilderness, along with hunting, fishing, and camping. I also learned from him that religion was not important. If a religious leader approached our home, my job was to distract the man so that my grandfather could leave the house by a back door.

When I was 12 years old, my heart was damaged by rheumatic fever. When I was 18, my heart got worse, and I was told I would need heart surgery. I was sad, angry, and frightened. Although my family was respected, they were not religious. Because of this they had no answers for my fear and the lack of peace in my soul. I found these answers in the Holy Bible.

Isaiah 41:10—God said, *"So do not fear, for I am with you; do not be dismayed, for I am your God. I will strengthen you and help you; I will uphold you with my righteous right hand."*

John 14:27—Messiah Jesus said, *"Peace I leave with you; my peace I give you. I do not give to you as the world gives. Do not let your hearts be troubled and do not be afraid."*

1 Peter 3:18—About Messiah Jesus it was said, *"For Christ died for sins once for all, the righteous for the unrighteous, to bring you to God. He was put to death in the body but made alive by the Spirit."*

In my hospital room waiting for surgery, I closed my eyes and spoke to God in prayer. I surrendered my life to Him through the name of Messiah Jesus and asked Him to give me new life. When I opened my eyes I knew that the spirit of Jesus had come to live inside me. For the first time I felt real peace and freedom from fear.

My physical heart seemed to get better for a time. However, 15 years later, while working in my office, my heart started beating wildly and my blood pressure dropped. As an ambulance took me to the hospital, I knew I was dying. Even so, I was experienced a tremendous peace and lack of fear. I remember speaking with Messiah Jesus, "Lord Jesus, I love you and appreciate you, and I am looking forward to being with you." Then my heart stopped completely.

By the skill of medical doctors and the grace of Almighty God, I was literally brought back to life from the dead. Today, as I continue in my submission to God, my greatest joy is to tell others that they too can have new life and peace and freedom from fear.

Praise be to God for His peace and deliverance from fear!

SUGGESTED READING LIST

BIOGRAPHIES

- *Beyond the Minarets: A Biography of Henry Martyn.* Waynesboro: STL Books, 1988.
- Chacour, Elias and David Hazard. *Blood Brothers.* Grand Rapids: Chosen Books, 1984.
- Chacour, Elias and Mary E. Jensen. *We Belong to the Land: The Story of a Palestinian Israeli Who Lives for Peace and Reconciliation.* University of Notre Dame Press, 2000.
- *Dr. Saeed of Iran: Kurdish Physician to Princes and Peasants, Nobles and Nomads.* Pasadena: William Carey Library, 1957.
- Sheikh, Bilquis and Richard H. Schneider. *I Dared to Call Him Father.* New Jersey: Fleming H. Revell Company, 1978.
- *The Torn Veil: The Story of Sister Gulshan Esther as Told to Thelma Sangster.* Fort Washington: CLC Books, 1984.
- Watt, W. Montgomery. *Muhammad: Prophet and Statesman.* New York: Oxford University Press, 1961.

MISCELLANEOUS

- Ali, A. Yusuf. *The Holy Qur'an.* Brentwood, Maryland: Amana Corporation, 1983.
- Arberry, Arthur John. *The Koran Interpreted.* New York: Simon & Schuster, 1955. www.simonsays.com.
- Elliot, Elisabeth. *These Strange Ashes.* New York: Harper & Row Publishers, 1975.
- Fernea, Elizabeth. *Guests of the Sheik: An Ethnology of an Iraqi Village.* New York: Doubleday, 1965.

- Issa, Fouad. *Al-Adha in the Injeel*. Indianapolis: Arab International Ministries, 1995.
- Jabbour, Nabeel. *The Rumbling Volcano: Islamic Fundamentalism in Egypt*. Pasadena: Mandate Press, 1993.
- Khan, Muhammad Muhsin. *The Translation of the Meanings of Sahih Al-Bukhari: Arabic-English*. Medina Al-Munawwara: Dar AHYA Us-Sunnah Al-Nabawiya, 2002.
- Mallouhi, Christine A. *Waging Peace on Islam*. Downers Grove: InterVarsity Press, 2000.
- Nouwen, Henri J.M. *The Return of the Prodigal Son: A Story of Homecoming*. New York: Doubleday, 1992.
- Von Grunebaum. *Classical Islam: A History 600–1258*. New York: Barnes and Noble, 1970.

OVERVIEW OF ISLAM
- Gilchrist, John. *Facing the Muslim Challenge: A Handbook of Christian-Muslim Apologetics*. Benoni: Muslim Evangelism Resource Centre of Southern Africa, 1999.
- Gilchrist, John. *The Qur'an: The Scripture of Islam*. Mondeor: Muslim Evangelism Resource Centre of Southern Africa, 1995.
- Miller, Roland E. *Muslim Friends: Their Faith and Feeling: An Introduction to Islam*. St. Louis: Concordia Publishing House, 1995.
- Miller, William M. *A Christian's Response to Islam*. Wheaton: Tyndale House Publishers, Inc., 1975.
- *New Paths in Muslim Evangelism: Evangelical Approaches to Contextualization*. Grand Rapids: Baker Book House, 1980.
- Parshall, Phil. *Inside the Community: Understanding Muslims Through Their Traditions*. Grand Rapids: Baker Book House, 1994.

PRACTICAL TOOLS
- Accad, Fouad Elias. *Building Bridges: Christianity and Islam*. Colorado Springs: NavPress, 1997.
- Crawford, Trudie. *Lifting the Veil: A Handbook for Building Bridges Across the Cultural Chasm*. Colorado Springs: Apples

of Gold, 1997.

- Marsh, Charles R. *Share Your Faith with a Muslim.* Chicago: Moody Press, 1975.

SPIRITUAL WARFARE

- Anderson, Neil T. *The Bondage Breaker.* Eugene, Oregon: Harvest House Publishers, 1995.
- Jabbour, Nabeel. *The Unseen Reality: A Panoramic View of Spiritual Warfare.* Singapore: The Navigators, 1995.
- Love, Rick. *Muslims, Magic, and Kingdom of God: Church Planting among Folk Muslims.* Pasadena: William Carey Library, 2000.
- Parshall, Phil. *Bridges to Islam: A Christian Perspective on Folk Islam.* Grand Rapids: Baker Book House, 1983.
- Wallis, Arthur. *God's Chosen Fast.* Christian Literature Crusade, 1993.
- Warner, Timothy L. *Spiritual Warfare: Victory over the Powers of This Dark World.* Westchester, Illinois: Crossway Books, 1991.

STORIES AND PROVERBS

- Arnander, Primrose and Ashkhain Skipwith. *Apricots Tomorrow: And Other Arab Sayings with English Equivalents.* London: Stacey International, 1985.
- Bailey, Kenneth E. *The Cross and the Prodigal: The 15th Chapter of Luke Seen Through the Eyes of Middle Eastern Peasants.* St. Louis: Concordia Publishing House, 1973.
- *Poet & Peasant: Through Peasant Eyes: A Literary-Cultural Approach to the Parables in Luke.* Grand Rapids: William B. Eerdmans Publishing Company, 1976.
- *The Son of a Duck Is a Floater: And Other Arab Sayings with English Equivalents.* London: Stacey International, 1985.

THE KING'S GIFT

Because stories play such an important role in Eastern culture, my wife wrote this as a gift for a dear Muslim friend. The story has since been shared with many other Muslims.

ONCE THERE LIVED A WISE AND GOOD KING. Many kinds of animals lived in his kingdom. The songbirds were his favorites. Each songbird sang a special melody that made the king very happy. The king told everyone that he would pay a high price to get more songbirds for his kingdom.

One day, some strangers traveling through the kingdom told the king about a beautiful bird. The bird had brilliant red and blue feathers. She sang the most beautiful melodies ever heard. But this bird lived far away. And she was imprisoned in a delicate golden cage. A bad government official owned the bird. When this man was angry, he would beat the bird's cage with a stick. The bird became frightened and confused. As a result, it only sang at night.

The king became angry when he heard this story. So he was determined to rescue the helpless bird. He told a trusted servant to find the bird and buy it. The servant gathered food and clothing for the long trip. He also filled a large sack with gold coins, for he was willing to pay a high price. So the servant left, riding on a strong horse.

Many weeks passed. Finally, on a warm spring day, the king's servant returned. He was holding the golden cage! He had a big smile on his face. He was glad to be home, because the journey had been difficult. And the government official had demanded a very, very high price.

Then the king took the golden cage to his lush garden, where he spent many hours enjoying the songs of the other birds that lived there. He carefully hung the cage on a branch of a tree, looking with great love and compassion at the frightened bird in the cage.

Then he did something strange. He opened the golden cage's tiny door. Then he walked away, because the bird was frightened. She was hitting her little body against the sides of the cage again and again.

When summer came, the beautiful bird was no longer afraid. This garden was a place of peace. The cage door was still open, but no one harmed her. No one beat on her cage anymore.

Every day she watched the gentle king as he walked in his garden. He spoke to the other birds, who were free, and didn't live in cages. He would pet them, too. Then the birds would sing back to the king!

All of these birds seemed so happy! Some of them were beautiful, and some were plain. Some were young, and some were old. But the king loved them all. He didn't notice their differences.

One day, a cheerful canary went to visit the bird in the golden cage. She flew through the open door, and sat down on the swing. Soon the two birds were friends. They talked about everything. The canary admired the fancy feeding dish and mirror. She had never seen such luxury! But the canary said there was something better: eating grain from the king's own hand. Sadly, the beautiful bird chose to eat alone in her cage.

They talked a lot about the open door. The bird in the cage explained to the canary that she had no desire to leave the cage, even though she was curious about life in the garden. Besides, all her relatives had been born and raised in cages. To her, they seemed happy.

The canary then patiently explained that the king was offering a wonderful gift. It was an invitation to fly! And she could even eat the best grain from the king's own hand. The canary also reminded her friend that the king had paid a very high price to bring her to his garden.

Every day the king held out his hand by the cage's door. He yearned for the little bird to come to him. But she was still afraid.

The king had perfect manners. He would never force her to leave the cage. He had simply opened the door of the cage. He patiently waited for her to fly out by herself. With all of his heart, the king wanted the bird to experience the love, joy, and peace that only he could give.

Several years passed. The happy canary still visited her friend often. But the imprisoned bird only sat in her cage. She seemed satisfied to watch the king through the bars of her cage. And the small golden door remained open.